HAGGADAH

A Celebration of Freedom

by Martha Shelley
with Hebrew translations by Ilana Brody

aunt lute books
SAN FRANCISCO

Cover Design: Emeline Mann Sanchez
Design and Typesetting: Emeline Mann Sanchez
Hebrew Typesetting: Ilana Brody
Senior Editor: Joan Pinkvoss
Managing Editor: Shay Brawn
Production Support: Tricia Lambie
                     Livia Tenzer
                     Shahara Godfrey
                     Corey Cohen

Printed in the U.S.A.

Aunt Lute Books
P.O. Box 410687
San Francisco, CA 94141

First Edition
10 9 8 7 6 5 4 3 2 1

Library of Congress Cataloging-in-Publication Data
Haggadah (Shelley)
     Haggadah : a celebration of freedom / by Martha Shelley ; with Hebrew translations by Ilana Brody.
     p. cm.
ISBN 1-879960-53-2 (paper)
     1. Haggadot—Texts. 2. Seder—Liturgy—Texts. 3. Judaism—Liturgy—Texts. 4. Feminism—Religious aspects—Judaism.
I. Shelley, Martha.
BM674.795.S54 1997
296.4'5371—dc21   97-36736
                                                    CIP

To my parents
Jacob Joseph Altman
and
Gitl Dina Bojankosky
who raised me in the tradition.

ACKNOWLEDGMENTS

I want to thank Amalia Bergman and Koré Grate for encouraging me to write this work, Debra DeBondt and Judy MacLean, who encouraged me to publish it; the Aunt Lute Manuscript Committee who brought it to the staff; Joan Pinkvoss and Shay Brawn of Aunt Lute Books, for kind and meticulous editorial work, and for transforming the DNA of the text into a newborn book with a physical presence in this world; Ilana Brody for her powerful Hebrew translation; and Deborah Lieberman for taking the time to vet the Hebrew.

I would also like to thank my friends who had the patience to listen to me read, and those who read the text on their own and gave me feedback—whether or not I agreed with their opinions. A writer, after all, is an odd duck who prefers to spend most of her time alone, struggling to paint pictures with words; it takes a special sort of person to befriend one.

Finally, a special thanks to you the reader, for whom this book was written and without whom it could not exist at all.

Introduction

What is Passover?

Passover is the holiday during which Jews celebrate the liberation of our people from slavery in Egypt — an event which may or may not have happened around 1200 B.C.E.. It is the spring festival, the time for renewal.

Haggadah means "the telling." The escape from Egypt is the defining legend, the central drama of the Jews. Every nation coalesces around such an epic; its people project themselves into the story, aspire to the virtues of its heroes, and through periodic retelling or dramatization, transmit their values to the next generation. To be a Jew is, among other things, to see yourself as having personally experienced the degradation of slavery and the journey to freedom.

Now perhaps you were raised in a different culture, never went to Bible class, or missed seeing *The Ten Commandments* (terrible acting — read the book instead). If so, here's the plot outline:

There was a famine in Israel. The patriarch Jacob emigrated to Egypt, where his son Joseph served as Pharaoh's economic advisor. Jacob's descendants kept their own customs and language (Hebrew), and multiplied so quickly that a later king grew uneasy over the alien presence within his own borders. He set them to hard labor under overseers who beat them when they didn't meet their quotas. Well, Pharaoh kept getting richer and his slaves kept having more children, so at last he ordered his soldiers to seek out any newborn male Hebrews and throw them into the Nile.

The infant Moses was saved from drowning by Pharaoh's own daughter. She adopted and raised him as a prince in the royal house. When he reached manhood he rejoined his people and became their spokesman, demanding that Pharaoh let them leave the country. Weeks of tough negotiations ensued. The king had his army and refused to give in; Moses had his God, who rained one plague after another on the nation of Egypt: blood, frogs, fleas, flies, cattle disease, boils, hail, locusts, darkness.

When fleas bit him or frogs swarmed in his bed, Pharaoh would agree to anything; as soon as the vermin died off he took it all back. Each pestilence was worse than its predecessor, until

"Hail" (Gurlitt: "The Ten Plagues," 1920).

God finally unleashed the Angel of Death. However, He first warned the Hebrews to mark their doorposts with lambs' blood so the Angel would pass over their homes (thus the name of the holiday, Passover). He also told them to pack everything they owned, take out loans from the Egyptians, and get ready to run.

At midnight the Angel flew over Egypt and slew the firstborn in all the unmarked homes — including the royal house. At this point every Egyptian wanted the Hebrews deported, and Pharaoh told Moses to take his people and be gone. They were dressed and ready, their bellies full of roast lamb.

Now comes the big chase. Imagine this raggedy mob, everyone from grandma to suckling babe marching out into the desert under the full moon. They've been in Egypt over 400 years and don't know how to fend for themselves, how to do anything but make bricks for Pharaoh. Instead of taking them due east along the main highway, which would bring them into conflict with the warlike Philistines, God leads them south; several days later they find themselves standing on the shore of

14th century Passover seder.

the Red Sea. By then Pharaoh has changed his mind yet again and sent out the slavecatchers.

The sea is before them, an army of cavalry and chariots at their backs. Then God parts the waves, letting the Hebrews pass between walls of water without even wetting the soles of their sandals. When the Egyptians try to follow, the walls collapse and drown them.

I've just omitted a wealth of dramatic detail and a whole cast of characters who save Moses' neck or the entire Hebrew people at crucial junctures: two midwives, Moses' mother, sister, brother, first wife and father-in-law. Notice that most of these are women (and let's not forget Pharaoh's daughter). Again I encourage you to read the original; it's a document of extraordinary power.

In Exodus (the Biblical book which describes these events) the Hebrews are told to celebrate the Passover for an entire week, during which they must abstain from leavened bread. On the first night they are to dress as though preparing for a journey. They must sacrifice an unblemished male lamb, then roast it whole and eat it with bitter herbs. And they must tell the story to their children as though they'd personally walked with Moses. Over the next 3,000 years these simple instructions developed into a complex ritual, layered with historic and spiritual meaning.

The Traditional Haggadah and How It Grew

If you go to a Jewish book store and ask for an Orthodox Haggadah, you will be handed a booklet in Hebrew, most likely with facing pages in the vernacular. What you'll have is a set of instructions for conducting the Passover celebration, interspersed with readings from the Bible, rabbinical commentaries, legends, prayers, hymns and children's songs. They represent three millennia of literary accretion — responses to theological debates, cultural developments, and changing political conditions.

By 200 C.E. the basic structure of the Haggadah was largely formed, and is described in some detail in a book of legal interpretations (the Mishnah). The oldest portions are Psalms 113 and 114, which were probably written within the lifetime of King David (1012-975 B.C.E.).

The Mishnah lists only three of the Four Questions traditionally asked by the youngest son during the seder. One of these was "On all other nights we eat meat roasted, stewed or cooked; why on this night only roast?" This is taken to mean that the questions were already in use during the period of the Second Temple (515 B.C.E.-70 C.E.), when the lamb was sacrificed there, taken home and roasted later. After the destruction of the Temple, the question "Why on this night do we eat reclining?" was substituted. The question about bitter herbs is a later addition.

The introductory statements, the reply to the Four Questions, and the popular hymn "Dayenu" seem to have originated during the 3rd century B.C.E., when Palestine was ruled by the Egyptian Ptolemaic dynasty. Biblical verses protesting oppression and invoking God's retribution were added during the Middle Ages in response to Church persecutions. An acrostic poem, "The Passover Seder is Complete," was appended in the 11th century, and the children's songs "Who Knows One" (*Ehad Ani Yode'a*) and "One Kid" (*HadGadya*) were first printed in Prague in 1590.

The earliest haggadot were included in prayer books rather than bound separately; individual volumes did not appear until the 12th century. Between the 13th and 15th centuries, wealthy patrons commissioned illuminated manuscripts for their families. Then in 1482 a press in Guadalajara issued the first printed Haggadah. Like its predecessors it was in Hebrew, the sacred language which God presumably spoke at Creation; translations did not come into use until the 16th century.

The first printed illustrated Haggadah. Prague, 1526.

Thousands of editions have been published since the invention of the printing press, most differing only slightly from the Orthodox. But no really significant attempts to change the liturgy were made until the 20th century. Then we who were the slaves of slaves rose up. Women began to demand inclusion in the story of our people's liberation. Now you can browse through that Jewish book store and find a Haggadah for almost any group that wants to hold a seder: women only, mixed egalitarian, gay and lesbian, New Age, vegetarian. And if none of them suit you, you can write your own.

Why is this Haggadah Different from All Others?

The traditional Haggadah is a dialogue between fathers and sons. This one is based predominantly but not exclusively on women's experience. While there are many feminist haggadot, I found that most of these retained too much of the orthodox liturgy for my taste, even when they gave God a sex change. Others spent time complaining about not being included in Jewish ritual, thus continuing to accept that male-defined ritual as primary. They end up being used on "alternate days" of the festive week, while the orthodox one is still used on the first and second nights of Passover and therefore remains the "real Haggadah" in the eyes of the celebrants.

All other haggadot, from the orthodox to the radically revisionist, were written for Jewish audiences. *Haggadah: A Celebration of Freedom* is a Passover seder for everyone. Though it is grounded in Jewish tradition, it draws on the struggles of many nations. It speaks of persistent heroism in the face of oppression—and also of the darkness in our souls that collaborates with Pharaoh. In a single tapestry it celebrates past victories, delineates the intricate patterns of tyranny and illuminates the paths of greatest resistance.

Almost all haggadot retain an image of God as distinct from the world, God as the Higher Power to Whom one addresses prayers. I tried to imbue this Haggadah with a Gaian sense of the divine, with the understanding that there is no separation between Spirit and Matter, between Creator and Creation. Therefore we cannot separate the spiritual and the political: if we try to do so we end up with religion as an opiate and politics as a Stalinist nightmare. Because we are one with God we are all holy, and the task of liberation becomes a *mitzvah*, a sacred duty.

"Women in the 1905 Revolution" (Sakhnorskaya)

Why Hebrew in this Text?

During the two millennia of exile, Hebrew was the link to our ancestors and to contemporary co-religionists; a Belgian and a Kazakh might not be able to communicate in any other way but they could pray together, could give each other shelter against periodic outbreaks of antisemitism. The ancient tongue connects many of us to childhood, festive meals and tiny cups of sweet red wine, the illusion of safety, of a benevolent deity watching over our family gathering. It also connects us with the modern state of Israel—another problematic family relationship.

So for reasons of history and nostalgia, I wanted a Hebrew text. There are, of course, the traditional Four Questions which children learn by heart. Then, Ilana Brody was kind enough to translate five poems: one for each of the four cups of wine, and one explaining the items on the seder plate. Unfortunately, we couldn't afford to have her translate the entire book, but hopefully those who know Hebrew will appreciate the beauty of her work.

How This Book Came Into the World

When I was a child I always wanted to ask the Four Questions, but I wasn't a youngest son or any kind of son at all. As I grew old enough to understand the rest of the text, I lost my desire to participate altogether. The traditional text barely notices the existence of women, mentioning us only three times: twice as mothers and once as the girl children spared by Pharaoh.

I also thought the Egyptian fellah got a raw deal.

My parents had been socialists in their youth, but the witch-hunts of the McCarthy era frightened them into silence. Yet they passed on their sense of ethics, compassion and concern for justice. When it was my turn to throw myself into the struggles of the day — anti-war, women's liberation, gay liberation — I had almost no historical perspective. My grandfather's mumbled Hebrew seemed the embodiment of conservatism rather than a prescription for resistance to tyranny.

And this is, after all, the spring festival. Prayers that might have been meaningful in centuries past seemed dry and repetitious, a soporific litany of praise to a distant deity, while my heart wanted to pour out song over every leaf and flower, to shout, God is right here!

I grew older, I had my heart broken personally and politically and took refuge in books. I needed to see my own successes and failures in a much broader context, so I began to study history, especially the history of my people.

In 1992 Dr. Amalia Bergman invited me to a feminist seder and asked me to contribute an explanation of the six items on the seder plate. A poem emerged, it was well-received, and Dr. Bergman suggested that I write an entire Haggadah. Too much work, I thought, and did nothing for the next three years; then out came "Song for the Angel of Death." In 1996 Sifu Koré Grate asked me to organize a seder for the Feminist Eclectic Martial Arts school in Minneapolis. Since most of her students knew nothing about Passover, I had a free hand, and a month to put it all together.

The task possessed me morning and evening, words bubbling up as from a hidden spring. I awoke to the knowledge that I had wanted to do this work for longer than I could remember, that it had been ripening in me until the moment when the gardener put her hand to the fruit and said, "Now."

How to Conduct a Passover Seder

Anybody can do it. You don't have to be Jewish to identify with the story of the exodus. Certainly African-Americans did. And the embattled women of Camp Sister Spirit held a seder on their Mississippi farm, surrounded by people who wanted to kill them. Hardly any Jews were present, but who can deny the validity of their offering?

Before the invention of the printing press, when books were hand-written and expensive, the average Jewish family celebrated at home, saying whatever prayers they remembered. A rhyme was devised to help them keep the order of the service:

> *Kadesh, urhatz, karpas, yahatz;*
> *maggid, rahtza, motsi matzah;*
> *maror, korech, shulhan orech;*
> *tzafun, barech, hallel, nirtzah.*

Here's a rough translation of the terms and description of the action:

Kadesh—*sanctify*. Bless the first cup of wine (or grape juice) and drink it.

Urhatz—*wash*. Wash your hands.

Karpas—*celery*. Dip greens in salt water and eat them.

Yahatz—*divide*. Break a matzah in two and hide part of it.

Maggid—*tell* (from the same root as haggadah). Tell the story. This part has a number of subsections and ends with a second glass of wine.

Rahtza—*wash* (same root as urhatz). Wash your hands again.

Motsi matzah—*bring forth*, as in God brings forth bread from the earth. Bless the matzah and eat a piece.

Korech—*bind, combine*. Make a sandwich of bitter herbs and matzah and eat it.

Shulhan orech—*long table*. Eat festive meal.

Tzafun—*hidden*. Find hidden piece of matzah and eat it.

Barech—*bless*. Say grace and drink a third cup of wine.

Hallel—*praise*. Praise God and drink a fourth cup of wine.

Nirtzah—*accepted*. Conclude the seder.

The week of Passover begins on the full moon in the Jewish month of Nisan. The Jewish calendar is lunar (each month begins with the new moon) and the day begins at sundown, not midnight. Consult your newspaper, synagogue, library or book store for the actual date. Jews outside Israel commonly have seders on the first two nights (in my family we ate with one set of grandparents on the first night and the other on the second); nowadays with both parents working outside the home, families are forced to celebrate on whatever Saturday night falls during that week. Some feminists also have a special women's seder on the last night.

You will need candles, wine or grape juice, and six items to put on the seder plate: 1) a roasted and scorched bone (vegetarians may substitute a broiled beet or "Paschal" yam); 2) a roasted egg; 3) parsley; 4) *haroset* (a mixture of chopped apples, nuts, wine and spices — different recipes are available); 5) bitter herbs (romaine lettuce, horseradish, endive or escarole); 6) three matzahs. The items on the seder plate aren't eaten, except for one matzah (the afikomen). You'll also need one hard-boiled egg per person, and enough parsley, bitter herbs, haroset, and matzahs so everyone can eat some, and small bowls of salt water for dipping.

As for the festive meal: you can obtain recipes for traditional dishes, or serve anything except leavened bread or foods made with leavening agents. Any foods which are not kosher are off limits; information about these dietary restrictions and the philosophy behind them is available from your library, synagogue or book store. Pork and shellfish are always off limits, and Jews may not eat meat and dairy products at the same meal. Your Jewish friends might break the rules on any other night but won't appreciate baked ham at a Passover dinner.

Gather your friends, prepare the seder plate, and take turns reading from this or any other Haggadah you like. Add whatever stories, poems or songs have significance for you. The journey to freedom is yours to take, the celebration yours to create.

HAGGADAH
A Celebration of Freedom

March 8, 1927, International Women's Day: 6000 women in Uzbekistan burn their veils in front of a mosque.

BEDIKAT HAMETZ - SEARCHING FOR LEAVEN

The night before the
full moon in Nisan, we
search the house for
all leavened products
and remove them
from our possession.
Traditionally this is the
culmination of a
general spring cleaning.

Because the winter rains
have washed the face of the earth
because the sun's love reaches
beyond its light to
waken burrowing creatures, to
burst seeds open in their furrows
because birds build new nests
a restlessness seizes us.
The earth itself urges us
to sweep the floors
burn the old straw in the fields
pour out the vinegared wine.

Because these are the days
of liberation, our souls
are driven to open the season
by casting out last year's leaven:

Here's a cupboard of rich cakes
for the fire, buttery torches
of pride, gifts we hoarded that died;
here are the challahs of contentment
here are two slices of the habits
of slavery squatting in
crumbs of resentment.

This bread was earned hard
this bread was begged from prison guards

this bread we spread our legs for
because we were needy or scared.

The old yeast won't work now, it's rancid
it shackles the heart to Mizraim
search for it with a candle
scrape out the crevices with knives
brush it away with feathers.
Let go of all your possession,
saying may it be like dust.

Yet when it burns it is a pillar of flame
cast it in water and it parts the sea
toss it to heaven, manna falls on us
all miracles arise from the dust of the earth,
from hametz.

Bruchot Habaot - Welcome

We introduce ourselves to one another, giving our first names followed by the names of our mothers and fathers.

Welcome. This is the full moon of Nisan, the first night of Passover. On this night we celebrate the deliverance of Israel from Mizraim. The name Israel means "one who wrestles with God"; it is a blessing and an inheritance. In each generation we must wrestle with the same questions and find new answers: What is the nature of the Divine? What does it mean to be human? What does it mean to be a Jew? What is freedom and how is it achieved?

4

Mizraim is the Hebrew name for Egypt. The rabbis say it means *in narrow straits*, because Egypt is a narrow fertile strip bounded on both sides by desert, and because our ancestors lived there under the constraints of slavery. But the Egyptian name for their country, Masr, means *the civilized place*, because Egypt was the mother of civilization. So perhaps we can begin to think about freedom by contemplating the constraints of our own civilization.

HADLAKAT NEROT - LIGHTING CANDLES

One person lights

the candles.

It all begins with light
the pulsations of stars
flung across black space

it begins with life eating
hot mud or frozen lichens,
or only stones
in the depths of the earth,

in the iron heart of the earth
not molten they tell us now
but immensely crystalline
six-sided like the bee's eye
six-sided like the star of Israel
singing with light

it begins with a word
that quivers like a candle
but will not be blown away
it erupts from the black
earth they grind you into

it begins with a
no *to pharaoh in his palace,*
no *to the pharaohs in pulpits and*
police stations, but first of all
no *to the pharaoh in the bedroom, and*
no *to whoever tells you*
you can't do without pharaoh

it begins with yes
to the bloody lips of truth,
yes *to the life in your belly,*
and yes *first of all to the light*
within you, even if they slay you
the light that on the day of your death
will bear you into
the world to come,
into the heart of the sun.

Fill your first cup with wine [or grape juice]. It is traditional to drink four cups of wine at the seder. Tonight with each cup we honor the many ways those who came before us have struggled for freedom. We drink in moderation — for remembrance, not for oblivion.

Woodcut of Harriet Tubman by WPA artist Elizabeth Catlett (1946).

לכבוד האם המלקטת בשדות כפופת גב
תחת משא השמש היוקדת.
ההודפת את המאיימים לחטוף שיבולת
מידיה הפצועות.
רגליה זבות דם אל האבק הסמיך
בעבור קומץ שיבולים עלובות,
חופן גרעינים לאפות ממנו לחם לילדיה.

לכבוד האם אשר הוציאה לחם
מעשב השדה ואוכל
מחלקי חזיר שהאדון השליך.
האם הכפופה מעל בטנה התפוחת.
גבה שותת דם
ושדיה נוטפות רק תפילה,
לילדיה המוצעים למכירה.

לכבוד האם אשר אספה את ילדיה
והסתירה אותם ביערות עד חלוף הפרעות.
ידיה כחולות וקרות כשלג ואפר שהיו ביתה,
עד האיר יום חדש
את גופו הקפוא של בנה בן היום.

For the mother who gleaned in the fields
back bent under the weight of the sun
shoving off those who would
snatch an ear of grain from her
bleeding hands, feet bleeding into
thick dust, for the sake of a handful
of ears of grain short of stalk and
empty of kernels, for the sake of a mouthful
of bread for her children;

for the mother who conjured up
nourishment from weeds and the parts
of a pig that the master cast aside,
for the mother bending over her
own swelling belly to pick cotton
whose back dripped blood,
whose breasts could only drip prayers
for the children auctioned away;

for the mother who snatched up
her children and hid in the forest
till the pogrom was over, till
her hands were blue as the snow
and the ashes that had been her home
were cold, till day broke over
the frozen body of her newborn son;

לכבוד האמהות אשר הסתירו את ילדיהם
במרתפים ובמנזרים.
האמהות שנשאו את ילדיהם, הבריחו גבולות
ופצצות נופלות מאחוריהם.

לכבוד אמהות הקוטפות קפה והשותלות אורז.
המנקות בתי שימוש, תופרות נעליים
או מלחימות שבבי סיליקון.
אמהות העובדות שתי משמרות
כדי לקנות ספרים וגם לחם לילדיהם,
אנו שותות.

ברוך פרי הגפן והאדמה,
ברוכים השמש והגשם.
ברוכות הידים אשר שתלו וזימרו.
ברוכות האמהות אשר נתנו לנו חיים
וגם קיימו אותנו.
ואשר בעמלן הגענו ליום הזה.
אמן.

for the mothers who hid their
children in cellars or convents
for the mothers who carried their
children across borders with
bombs falling behind them;

for the mothers picking coffee or planting rice
cleaning toilets or sewing sneakers
or soldering silicon chips;
for the mothers who work two shifts
to buy books as well as bread
for their children; we drink.

Blessed is the fruit of the vine
and the earth and the sun and the rain,
and the hands that planted and pruned.
Blessed are the mothers who gave us life and
sustained us, and whose labor enabled us to
reach this occasion. Amen.

URHATZ - WASHING THE HANDS

Wash your hands in silent meditation. Empty your mind of irrelevant thoughts; open your heart to your companions.

KARPAS - DIPPING THE GREENS

Take a green vegetable

(but not a bitter one)

and dip it into saltwater.

Why do we dip karpas in salt water? Karpas is for renewal. It stands for our ability to reach beyond what we thought possible, not just in the springtime but on every morning of our lives. It reminds us that each generation must repair and renew the world. They say salt water is for the tears of our ancestors in bondage; we say it is also for the sea that spawned all life.

Say the blessing, then

eat the karpas.

Praise the green things
that thicken flesh and bone
praise the seed and the leaf that hold
the secrets of healing
praise the season of quickening.

YACHATZ - BREAKING THE MIDDLE MATZAH

There are three matzot on the seder plate, covered with a cloth. We break the middle matzah in two, hide the larger section (called the afikomen), and place the smaller section between the two unbroken matzot. This is done as a silent meditation, to remind us that what we know is less than what is hidden from us. We hope to find the afikomen before the end of the seder meal, just as we hope to find the wisdom that makes us whole before the end of our lives.

MAGGID - TELLING THE LEGEND

We turn down the covering on the matzot, lift up the seder plate and say: This is the bread of ancient hospitality. We ate it when we lived in the desert in tents, and none was greater than her neighbor. Let all who are hungry come and eat. Let whoever is alone come and share our Passover. This year we are in exile. Next year, in our own land. This year we are slaves. Next year, may we all be free.

Now we are enslaved because a few have plenty, and many lack enough to eat. We are enslaved because we labor in fear of losing the little we have, and because fear makes us turn our backs on those who have less.

In this place of exile we are told to give charity, but it is never enough, because we forget that the word *caritas* means love and we give with pity but without love. The Hebrew

U.S. women stand with **Women in Black**, Jerusalem
(Photo: Penny Rosenwasser, 1989).

13

מה נשתנה הלילה הזה מכל הלילות.
שבכל הלילות אנו אוכלין חמץ ומצה.
הלילה הזה כולו מצה.
שבכל הלילות אנו אוכלין שאר ירקות.
הלילה הזה מרור.
שבכל הלילות אין אנו מטבילין אפילו פעם אחת.
הלילה הזה שתי פעמים.
שבכל הלילות אנו אוכלין בין יושבין ובין מסובין.
הלילה הזה כולנו מסובין.

words for this giving are *tzedaka,* or justice, and *nedivot,* or generosity. So in order to achieve liberation we need love, and a generous spirit, and a passion for justice.

The Four Questions

These are the traditional questions asked by the youngest child:

Why is this night different from all other nights?

On all other nights we eat hametz or matzah. On this night, only matzah.

On all other nights, we eat any vegetables. On this night we eat bitter herbs.

On all other nights we do not dip even once. On this night, we dip twice.

On all other nights we eat sitting upright or reclining. On this night, we all recline.

And these are the questions behind the questions:

How did we become enslaved?

How shall we become free?

The broken piece of the middle matzah is uncovered and the story is told as a response. We were slaves to Pharaoh in Egypt. A wind came out of the wilderness bearing the divine aroma of freedom, and the spirit of the people rose up to meet it. They put down the trowels that they used to lay bricks for Pharaoh's storehouses, they abandoned their ovens and stewpots. And if our ancestors had not possessed the courage to walk away from the familiar, to cross the Sinai desert in the dark of night, we and our children and grandchildren would still be slaves in Egypt.

We went out of Egypt but after a few generations the Assyrians came down and conquered us, and then the Greeks and then the Romans. We were torn on the racks of the Inquisition, beaten in the Czar's army, worked without a sabbath in the textile mills of America. We became the ashes of slaves in the Fuhrer's ovens. Yet each time the legend of our deliverance sustained us and gave us the courage to fight our oppressors. Therefore, it is incumbent on us to tell our children the story of each Exodus, to guide them when they embark on their own journeys. And whoever teaches her children the truth of her own struggle, withholding nothing, that woman is worthy of praise.

How did we become enslaved?

It began with an ambitious man, a clever man, a schemer who dreamed of ruling over his brothers instead of a handful of sheep. Now Joseph was his father's favorite, son of the favorite wife, but he was young then and couldn't hold his tongue about these outrageous fantasies, and he drove his older brothers to smoldering rage. So they stripped him of the fancy coat he used to dance around the pasture in, threw him in a pit and sold him down the Nile.

Even in chains Joseph was keen, and lucky too: he was bought by Pharaoh's chamberlain, who saw the boy had brains and promoted him to overseer. His career would've ended there, except the mistress said he tried to rape her. It's an old story, the woman against the slave. Joseph's folks insisted she was a floozy who made false accusations, but the owner of the plantation believed his wife, and our lad landed in a cell.

Even in the house of detention Joseph did well. His cleverness came to Pharaoh's attention and got him another promotion, a big one this time: to govern all of Mizraim. Now here was his scheme: he told Pharaoh to raise taxes in the good years and sell the grain when times were lean, when hungry farmers would give up their horses, cattle, land, even everything they had for a loaf of bread.

So all the land became Pharaoh's and all the Egyptians his bondmen; nowadays we call them sharecroppers. But Joseph bargained for his kin and when a famine came to Canaan, Pharaoh let the Hebrews have a rich piece of Egypt to pasture their sheep.

Then Joseph died. Another king took the throne and disowned the treaty, as rulers do when it suits their convenience. "We've got too many Hebrew immigrants," he said. And he named new taskmasters to lash those shepherds into brickyard gangs, to make them build enormous storehouses, to hold the overflow of grain that only Pharaoh owned.

How do we become enslaved?

We are ambitious for special privileges; we want to lord it over our companions. We resent the talents of others and slander them. We want someone else to do the dirty jobs, the dangerous jobs, someone else to work long hours at low wages so that we might live in luxury. We sell our talents to pharaohs in the hope of advancement. We let other nations be enslaved in the hope that we will be spared.

We're afraid and we clamor for protection — from soldiers, husbands or hooligans — so we sell ourselves into protection rackets. We're slothful: we want others to study and decide, to manufacture our desires, even to write the scripts of our dreams.

We walk in darkness whenever we fail to see the divine light in a human soul.

How shall we become free?

We begin with the word — the legend passed down.

The Four Children

The traditional haggadah teaches the father how to instruct four sons: one wise, one wicked, one simple, one who does not know how to ask. The wise son asks for laws and commandments — but what does the wise daughter say?

She asks questions, more than four, more than a thousand; they dance like dragonflies. She wants to know what you have done, to admire it in her youth and surpass it in her maturity. Her questions fill your eyes with wonder, they tear through the curtains of your pain. The wise daughter dangles upside-down from branches, overturning the old laws; she fills your heart with fear for her safety. What can you tell her? Let her climb on your shoulders; she will be your teacher.

The wicked son says, What does this service mean to *you?* and cuts himself off from his people. What does the wicked daughter say?

She tears at your pain and mocks it, believing she herself was not made like other women. She disparages her ancestors because they labored in slavery. The sustenance you offer never suffices because your lowly status taints your gifts, but she scrambles after men's leavings. She thinks she can cross the desert alone, but all she finds is loneliness. How can you teach her? Let her not join the seder till she realizes that she needs every woman present to make the journey with her.

The Orthodox forbid women to pray together in groups, to pray out loud, and to hold a Torah. These women gathered to pray at the Western Wall in Jerusalem, and were asaulted by the Orthodox men; their case is still pending in the Israeli Supreme Court: (l to r) Rifka Haut, Phyllis Chesler, Rabbi Helene Ferris and Susan Aronoff (Photo: Joan Roth).

What does the simple daughter say?

Like the wise son, she asks for commandments. She wants to make her journey in your footsteps. What can you tell her? Each day you must give a little less than she demands, letting her weave the missing strands herself.

And the one who doesn't know how to ask?

Lead her to the table and give her a place of honor. She was forced to be silent; now you must draw her out, you must ask her questions and give her time to find her voice. The seder will not be complete, and the Children of Israel will not be free, without this fourth child.

A Fifth Question from the Children

We've heard of four types of daughters but not of the mothers. Why are all the mothers in our legend wise, enduring and strong — were there no wicked mothers?

There were and there are: mothers who drink themselves insensible while the fathers go to their daughters' beds. The poorest of the poor, who prostitute the girls to feed the rest of the family; and those who sell their children for liquor or drugs. Crippled mothers who cripple their daughters to please prospective husbands: breaking and binding the foot, slicing off the sexual parts. Or those who simply amputate the soul, whose harshness is forever turned against the female child.

The Hebrews were slaves in Mizraim for 430 years; men began to enslave women at least 4,000 years ago, and we've only begun to dream of an Exodus. Too often we've had to survive by collaboration, and every woman's hand has at least a drop of woman's blood on it. When we begin

Muslim Palestinian women in Jerusalem Peace March (Photo: Penny Rosenwasser, 1989).

Women in Black, Belgrade (Photo: Vesna Pavlović).

to understand the magnitude of this history of betrayal, our tongues go numb, our hands hang nerveless by our sides. We know why trust is so hard to earn, so fragile, and yet so desperately desired; we're awed by the persistent miracle of women's friendships.

Tze u'lmad - Go and learn

Tze u'lmad, the rabbis tell us, Go and learn. It is written, "your ancestors went down into Mizraim with 70 individuals." These were Joseph and his brothers and their sons, and the men who wrote this story did not count the sisters and daughters as individuals. We struggle to remember them, our throats ache to utter the names of the forgotten. Through them the children of Israel multiplied and filled the land.

The king of Egypt enslaved us, and when he feared our bondage was not harsh enough, he ordered the newborn sons slain, but allowed the girls to live. We remember that Pharaoh did women no favors; he was just culling the herd. The girls were saved to be raped, to be breeders of slaves.

It is written that God saw our suffering, that God heard our cries and sent Moses to tell the king to release us. And in order to demonstrate his own power, God hardened Pharaoh's heart, so that it was necessary to send ten plagues on Egypt, to make the Egyptians suffer because their king made others suffer, to loosen his grip long enough for the Hebrews to escape in the dark of night.

We wonder what kind of person imagined such a god, a god who needs to demonstrate his power by making others suffer? Who made a god in the image of Pharaoh?

The Ten Plagues

Maybe old Egypt was lucky after all
so what if the Nile stank of blood for a week?
year after year our rivers
run excrement, effluent,
*   profit and poison*

the Egyptians scratched lice
and slapped at gnats
and when locusts devoured the crops
they netted the critters and
fried 'em for dinner
we're fool enough to poison the bugs
the birds that eat them
and our wheat as well

their cattle died and frogs overran
the land; our cattle overgraze
we burn down the forests to feed them

**Demonstration against the Gulf War in San Francisco
(Photo: Penny Rosenwasser, 1991).**

*we've developed chemicals
that eat the sky and kill
all the pretty little amphibians
our frogs are rarer than princes*

*they had boils and we have AIDS
they had hailstorms but
everyone gets some bad weather*

*we could bear the blows
of heaven and earth
even endure a child's death
bear all evils but the two
that cause most misery:
human greed
and human cruelty.*

Here it is customary to sing the Dayenu, to give thanks for 15 divine blessings our nation received. Five of these were acts of vengeance against the Egyptians; five were acts of liberation necessary to bring us from Mizraim to the land of Israel; five were cultural gifts that made us a people. The recitation of each act is a verse and the chorus is Dayenu — "it would have been enough for us," i.e., if God had done any one of these things. Some progressive Jews omit the acts of vengeance. Some substitute a list of unfinished tasks, injustices that need to be rectified. In this Haggadah we save the blessings for later; now we consider our own capacity for inflicting suffering.

Song for the Angel of Death

On this night the lintels drip
with lamb's blood;
on this night we were taught to praise, dayenu,
the god who slew the sons of the mothers
of Mizraim, someone else's sons;
on this night we were taught to pray for
the Angel of Death to pass our doors.
Now we say, throw open the shutters,
confront him, call him in.

Mel'akh ha mavet, good evening.
Don't be a stranger.
Long ago somebody hired you
*   to teach the children.*
You live here, you squat in the corner
*   and fatten on secrets.*
You perch on the rim of a wound
*   and lap up shame like molasses, like pus.*

You guide our tongues to slander
  whoever we think has more, or better,
  whoever rejects our desire.
You guide our eyes to despise
  whoever is most like us.
You deafen our ears to the cries
  of someone else's children,
you instruct our bellies to hunger
  for crumbs from those who despise us.

And when crumbs and all your teachings
leave us empty, lonely, betrayed,
  suffused with memories of pogroms,
  our mothers driven to madness,
  our nation driven to weave an aggadah
  of blood revenge and liberation,
in the darkest night of our pain
you direct our hearts to murder
as if blood would drown shame.

Mel'akh ha mavet, come in.
Sit down by the fire, in the light.
On this night especially
  we need to keep on eye on you.

THE SEDER PLATE

Six items are traditionally present on the seder plate. Each has a meaning, but perhaps that significance has changed over the two millennia of our wanderings. Once we lived among the Persians, whose New Year falls at the spring equinox, who place

כרפס, פטרוסייליה, סלק, כרפס,
מסמל את כל הירק
הצומח מתוך האדמה השחורה
עולה מתוך גשמי החורף
ירוק הבוקע סלעי גרניט
ופורץ מעלה לינוק קרני שמש לוטפת.

ביצה, הביצה היא העולם,
מקור חיים בלתי נדלה.
העושר העגול של הבריאה.
מדוע ביצה מבושלת, צלויה בתנור?
אומרים הרבנים:
סמל לקורבן
אשר הביאו אבותינו לבית המקדש.

אנו אומרות:
ביצה היא לזכר הנשים שהוקרבו ונשכחו.
נשים אשר נשמטו מרשימות אין סוף
של גברים חסרי ביצית אשר הולידו עוד גברים.

six items on a special cloth, eat eggs and greens, and decorate
the house with sprouted wheat in mummy-shaped planters to
represent the resurrection of Osiris. And Babylonian Osiris is
Tammuz, whose month we celebrate in summer; we were cap-
tive in Babylon and adopted its calendar. Yet aside from the calendar, it's often impossible to tell which customs we learned
from our neighbors, which they learned from us, and which
have their roots in a common pagan past, a time before nations,
before slavery and war.

First:

Karpas, *parsley, celery,*
we celebrate all green things
that spring from black earth
spring from long-awaited winter rains
green that splits granite
and thrusts up to suckle the sun.

Second:

Beitzah, *the egg, the world egg, ha'olam,*
the endless beginning of life,
rich round of creation.
Why is it roasted in the oven?
The rabbis say, it stands for the sacrifice
        brought to the Temple,
they say it stands for the Temple's destruction.

We say it is a remembrance
        of women sacrificed and forgotten,
women omitted from endless lists of eggless men
        who begat other men.

לזכר הראשים החרוכים של נשים משוררות
אשר פתחו את דלתות התנורים והציתו בהם אש.
לזכר הנשים שנשרפו בתנורי אושביץ,
ביצים מנועות מבקיעה לצפורים מנועות משירה.

זרוע, עצם צלויה עם מעט בשר,
עצם טלה, בן האביב, יציר כל חי.
שה הפסח, בן בכור, נלקח משד,
חלב אימו עדין רטוב על שפתיו,
דם קורבנך נוטף ממשקופי הדלתות
להרוות צמאונו של מלאך המוות.
דמך נוטף מהמזבח, מהכידון ומהחור שפער הכדור.

הרבנים אומרים:
זכר ליד אלוהים
כי ביד חזקה הוצאנו אלוהים מעבדות לחירות.
אנו אומרות:
רק כאשר נעמוד נגד כל הפרעונים,
הכוהנים והנשיאים המקריבים את בנינו,
רק אז נעלה על הדרך המובילה מעבדות לחירות.

חרוסת, תפוחים ואגוזים מרוסקים מעורבים ביין,
פרי עמלנו בכרם ובבוסתן, טעמו מה מתוק הטעם.

A remembrance of parched heads of women poets
who opened the ovens and turned on the gas,
women shoved into ovens at Auschwitz and gassed,
eggs forbidden to hatch into
birds forbidden to sing.

Third:
Z'roa, roasted bone with bits of meat,
lamb bone, spring born,
the creation of all flesh.

Paschal lamb, first born son taken
from your mother's breasts,
lips still dripping with milk,
your sacrificed blood drips from the doorposts
to slake the thirst of the Angel of Death,
blood drips from the altar, from the bayonet,
the bullet hole.

The rabbis say this bone stands for the mighty arm
of god who led us out of bondage.
We say, only when we stand against the pharaohs,
the priests, the presidents
who lead our sons to be sacrificed
only then will we begin
to lead ourselves from bondage.

Fourth:
Haroset, chopped apples and nuts mixed with wine,
fruit of our labor in vineyard and orchard.
Taste it, it's sweet.

חרוסת היא הטיט והלבנים שעשינו לפרעה,
הפרוכות שרקמו נשים שנאסר עליהן לגעת בתורה.
היא המדים שתפרו הנשים במחנות ההשמדה,
הספרים שנכתבו בידי נשים אך פורסמו בשם בעליהם.
היא גופן של נשים שנמכרו לנשואין ולזנות.

הלילה אנו מברכות על פירותינו שלנו,
פודות את רכושנו שנגזל.
הלילה נזכור היותנו רכוש.

מרור, חזרת, ימים מרים של עבדות.
מרור יקר מתכשיטים,
מרור הוא זכרון, אין חרוסת בלעדיו.
בעבור מרור חייבת כל אישה לספר את סיפור אימה,
לספר את האמת שלה עצמה ללא בושה.

הרבנים אומרים:
דבר כאילו אתה עצמך היית עם משה,
כאילו אתה עצמך יצאת ממצריים.
אנו אומרות:
אין זה "כאילו", זה אכן קורה עכשיו.
בכל דור ודור רודפים אותנו
המשעבדים, המגיפות והפרעות.
דבר מרור! תן לכל קול אישה
להוביל את בנותיה
ולהוציאן מן המדבר.

This is the mortar we made for pharaoh
these are torah covers, embroidered
    by women forbidden to touch the torah,
these are garments sewn by women
    in the Triangle Shirtwaist Factory,
books written by women and claimed by their husbands,
bodies of women sold into marriage or prostitution.

Tonight we feast on our own fruit,
    reclaim our stolen property;
tonight we remember being *property.*

Fifth:
Maror, *bitter herbs, horseradish,*
    bitter days of slavery.
Maror is more precious than jewelry,
maror is memory, there is no haroset
    without it.
For the sake of maror, each woman
    must tell her mother's story,
    must speak her own truth without shame.

The rabbis say, speak as though you were there
    with Moshe, as though you personally
    were led from Mizraim.
But we say, it is not "as though", it is now.
In each generation the slavemasters come for us,
    the plagues, the pogroms.
Speak maror. Let each woman's voice
    guide her daughter through the wilderness.

מצה, מדוע קוראים הרבנים למצה "לחם צער"?
מצה איננה לחם עבדות
ולא ניתנה למאכל תחת הצלפות הרודן.
אמותינו אפו את הלחם הזה.
הוא לא הספיק ל"עלות",
הוא נתן את העליה לבני ישראל
אשר עלו לפני עלות השחר וחמקו.
נתן לאישה המוכה שהבריחה את ילדיה עם שחר.
לאישה שהושתקה ואשר החלה להרים קולה,
לאישה שנאנסה והרימה את אגרופה נגד התוקף,
לאישה הלוחמת, לאישה הפליטה.
רוח המצה חודרת אל תוך לחמן בכל מקום.
זהו לחם החירות.

Black women in Bloemfontein, South Africa protesting against the carrying of passes by women in 1913. (Photo Cape Archives, ref VA3468.)

Sixth:

Matzah.

Why do the rabbis call it, "bread of affliction"?
This isn't slave bread,
    pharaoh's wages, eaten under the lash.
Our mothers made this bread.
It could not rise, it gave its rising
to the Children of Israel
    who rose before dawn, who stole away
to the battered woman who rose before dawn
    who stole her children away
to the silenced woman who began to raise her voice
to the raped woman who raised her fist
to the striker, to the refugee
the spirit of matzah enters their bread, everywhere.
This is the bread of freedom.

Second Kadesh

Fill your second cup.
Our first cup was for the mothers. With this cup we consider the women of learning.

In the beginning learning was synonymous with motherhood. This is one of those simple truths, so obvious that men have labored for centuries to bury it. And this is a simple story, but one that needs repetition, needs to be shouted against the hurricane of lies howling around us. Whoever tells it at length, whoever elaborates on it, is worthy of praise.

Man proceeds from woman's womb, not woman from man's rib. Women gave us the mother tongue: it was we, not Adam, who named the animals.

Women are the mothers of invention: we put seeds in the ground nearest our homes so we wouldn't have to spend so much time foraging. The first chemists, we invented cookery; and in our cookpots brewed perfumes and medicines, made soap, tanned leather, dyed fibers. The first engineers, we stretched skins across branches and made tents; our desert ancestors knew that the tent belonged to the woman and the divorced man returned to his mother.

Then came the patriarchal revolution: men usurped power and monopolized knowledge. What was freely given became enslaved information, carefully guarded, subject to hierarchies of cruelty. An ancient scribe wrote, "A boy's ears are on his back. If you beat him, he will learn." During the last two millenia, the rabbis systematically excluded women from learning Torah, from forming study groups or taking positions of leadership in the community.

These rabbis also said, "Who fails to educate his son, teaches him to be a thief." And we can add what they dared not say, confront them with their guilt: "Who fails to educate a daughter, teaches her to be a whore — whether to one man or a thousand."

And today the usurpers seek to extend their power in previously inconceivable ways. They write laws giving them the right to patent plants that native women have used for centuries, they map and patent the genes in every living cell. These modern pharaohs won't rest content with storehouses of grain, they want to own your chromosomes. We will need to do more than march across the Sinai to defeat them.

Brown Brothers Clothing Worker's Strike, NYC 1912.

לכבוד הנשים המשכילות, בנות המזל,
אלה אשר הוריהם העניקו להם,
לימדו אתן מוסיקה ושפות,
ושלחו אותם למיטב האקדמיות.
לכבוד הנשים אשר ההורים לא נתנו להם מאום
מלבד תיאבון אין סוף.
אלה שעסקו בעבודות בזויות
וקראו ספרים אל תוך הלילה.
אלה שהמתינו מחוץ לאולמי ההרצאות
בשעה שגברים צעירים חלפו על פניהם
מדיפים ריח קולון וארוחת ערב דשנה.
נשים אשר ויתרו על ארוחות ותרופות
כדי לשלם שכר לימוד
והקשיבו רפות מרעב ומחלות.

לכבוד האישה
שלקחה את אשר למדה ופתחה בית ספר.
שקיבצה כסף עבור ספרים.
שלימדה לבושת מעיל חורף כאשר אזל הפחם.
שחסכה בדלי סבון וגיר.
לכבוד הנשים שהעזו להתווכח,
לכתוב ספרים ולחשוב.
לכבוד הנשים אשר דרשו יותר מאמהות,
אנו שותות.

תבורכנה הנשים הקוטפות פרי מהעץ האסור,
החוטפות ענפים מוכי ברק והמשחקות באש.
תבורכנה המורות היודעות כי נשמות אינן עצם דומם,
אלה המציתות את הדור בלהבה.
אמן.

For the women of learning, the lucky,
whose parents made provision, taught them
music and languages, sent them to
better academies
for women whose parents gave them nothing
but the keenest appetite,
who worked at menial jobs and read into the night
who waited outside the lecture halls
while young men strode in past them
bearing the scent of cologne and
lamb chop dinners
women who skipped meals and medicine
to pay tuition, who listened
faint with hunger and fever

for the woman who took what she learned, however
she got it, and opened a school
who begged money for books
and taught in her overcoat when
she ran out of coal, who saved
soap chips and string and chalk
for women who dared to talk back and
write books and think
for women who demanded more than motherhood,
we drink.

Blessed are the women who tear fruit from forbidden
trees, who snatch up the branches struck by lightning
and play with fire. Blessed are the teachers who know
that souls are not dead wood, who kindle them and set
a generation ablaze.   Amen.

Rahtza - Washing the Hands

This is the second washing of the hands, done in preparation for eating the festive meal. A blessing accompanies it.

With this washing we remember the women who carried water from the wells, and who still struggle under the weight of water jars in many parts of the world. We remember the hospitality of the desert: whenever travelers arrived, the women of the household went out first with pitchers to slake their thirst, and the thirst of their animals.

Motsi Matzah - Blessing the Matzah

One person picks up the matzot on the seder plate and says:

Blessed are the farmers who plant and tend and reap, who bring forth bread from the earth. Blessed are the bakers who labor all night to give us our daily bread. They are the cornerstones of the temple, the pillars of our dreams.

Put down the broken piece, and break up the two whole matzot and distribute them. Each participant should eat a piece of matzah while reclining on the left side.

Maror

Each person takes a portion of maror.

We can't bless bitterness; there's nothing sacred about our suffering, or the suffering of our people. We bless instead those friends who helped us through bitter times, who gave us a meal

"Ruth" by E.M. Lilien.

Ruth gleaning the sheaves.

**"And when ye reap the harvest of your land, thou shalt not wholly reap the corner of thy field....
And thou shalt not glean the vineyard...Thou shalt leave them for the poor and for the strangers...." Lev. 19:9-10.**

or a place to sleep or a new job; and those who helped us bury our dead. May they live long and be graced with an easy passing.

Eat the maror but do not recline, because maror is a symbol of slavery.

KORECH - THE HILLEL SANDWICH

One person takes the piece of the third matzah (the one that was broken at the beginning of the seder) and makes a sandwich with maror and haroset.

Hillel was head of the rabbinic academy in Jerusalem during the Roman domination. He created this sandwich to follow the Biblical injunction, "They shall eat it with matzot and bitter herbs." Very little is known of his life, except a handful of sayings.

We are told that a Roman came to him and demanded that he teach the entire Law while standing on one foot. He replied, "Don't do to another what would be hateful to you. That is the whole Torah. The rest is commentary."

The tales of Hillel are sweet, but we are left to wonder, with the cynicism of slaves whose humanity has long been disregarded, even in that same Torah which he followed so literally — How did he treat the women of his family? The servants in his household? Why are men like Hillel and Jesus honored as great sages when they "discover" the basic truths that every mother must teach her small children?

Perhaps we should eat Hillel sandwiches every day as a reminder; perhaps women who cook for men should serve them at every meal; perhaps every boss and bureaucrat should eat nothing but Hillel sandwiches until those words become flesh and bone.

Eat the Hillel sandwich while reclining.

SHULHAN ORECH - THE FESTIVE MEAL

We begin by eating an egg dipped in salt water, as all things begin with the egg; then it is customary to eat the rest of the meal. (We can also eat the egg as a symbol of the meal, finish the ritual, then feast and socialize.) After eating, the children should look for the afikomen.

TZAFUN - EATING THE AFIKOMEN

Each person eats a small piece of the afikomen, while reclining. The entire afikomen should be consumed without pause or interruption, as an act of meditation. Think about what intellectual or spiritual or emotional qualities you will seek to develop in the coming year. At the end of the evening, the child who found the afikomen is given a small reward.

Ya`el kills Sisera. Sisera the Canaanite general fled after losing a battle to the Israelites. Ya`el invited him into her tent, gave him milk to drink, and when he fell asleep she drove a tent stake through his skull.

BARECH - GRACE

Fill the third cup of wine.

Our third cup is for the woman warrior.

תפילה אל האלה הכנענית הבתולה ענת
אשר קשרה ראשים כרותים על גבה
וחגרה ידים כרותות למותניה
אשר צהלה בדמים.

לכבוד השומרים אשר נצטוו להגן על
מיתחם הנשים בטירת האביר,
בעת שהתאמנו בחרבות
פגיונות או נאגאנאתה
עד אשר היתה האדמה תחתיה
רטובה ועיניה צרבו מזעה.

לכבוד האישה שנאלצה
להשתמש במיניותה להגן על עמה.
לכבוד יעל מפתה את סיסרה
ותוקעת יתד ברכתו.
לכבוד יהודית מפתה וכורתת
את ראשו של הולופרנס
לכבוד הנשים האלג'יריות
אשר בגלל מינן נראו בלתי מסוכנות,
ולכן עברו את עמדת הבקורת
כשהן נושאות מטעני חבלה
תחת שיפולי הג'לביה
קרוב לליבן הפועם.

לכבוד האישה שנאלצה
להתעלם ממינה ולהגן על עמה,
אשר התעוררה קפואה
משינה על האדמה הקרה,
אשר רצה לעשות את צרכיה
בטרם יעיר השחר
את בושתה בפני חבריה.
מגחכת למשמע בדיחותיהם הבזויות

An invocation:
to the goddess of Canaan, the maiden `Anat
who bound severed heads to her back
who wore a belt of severed hands
who exulted in blood.

For the guard commanded
to defend the women's quarters
or the lord's castle, who
practiced with shortsword
or dagger or naginata till
the earth beneath her was wet
and sweat stung her eyes

for the woman compelled
to use sex to defend her people,
Yael seducing Sisera and
pounding a stake through his temple
Yehudit seducing and beheading
Holofernes, for Algerian women
whose sex made them seem harmless,
passing through checkpoints
carrying plastic explosives
under billowing djellabas
next to their hammering hearts

for the woman compelled
to deny her sex to defend her people,
who woke up stiff
from sleeping on damp ground
and ran to relieve herself
before reveille sounded
before dawn revealed
her secret to her comrades
smiling at their jokes

על חלקי גוף נשי,
סועדת איתם ארוחת בוקר חצי מבושלת
ומאותו שיכר קלוקל שואבת אומץ
לצעוד בשדות הדגן הרמוסים.
צרחות הפצועים
מפלחות את ענני עשן אבק השריפה.
שינים נוקשות תפילה לנצחון או מות מהיר.

לכבוד נשים שקטלו זרים
ואטמו אוזניהן מלשמוע
בכיים של אמהות אחרות.
אשר בשתיקתם
חיפו על אחיהן
שאנסו בנות עם אחר.
לכבוד נשים אשר באומץ ליבן
שיחררו את בעליהן,
אשר הודו להן בכך ששלחו אותן
חזרה למטבח.

לכבוד נשים שלחמו להגנתן.
לכבוד אינז גארסיה, שירתה
באחד הגברים שאנסוה.
נשפטה פעמיים לבסוף שוחררה.
רק אחרי שמכרה את ביתה כדי לשלם
לעורכי הדין.
לכבוד פולן דבי אשר ירתה והרגה
עשרים ושנים בני כסטה עליונה
אשר אנסוה.
היא נכלאה ושוחררה
אחרי שרופאי הכלא
כרתו את רחמה.
לכבוד נשים שהרגו
את בעליהם או חבריהם שאנסו אותן
ועדין כלואות בבתי סוהר.

about the body parts of women
sharing their half-cooked breakfast
and bad whiskey nerving her up
to march over trampled wheat
and the screaming wounded
firing through clouds of gunsmoke
at indistinct figures
teeth chattering over a prayer
for victory or quick death

for women who slew strangers,
who shut their ears to another
mother's wails, whose silence
covered their brothers' rape
of another nation's daughters
whose courage freed their men
who thanked them and sent them
back to the kitchen

and women who fought for themselves:
for Inez Garcia, who shot one
of the men who raped her
and was tried twice and freed
at last, after losing her home
to pay lawyers
for Phoolan Devi, who shot
twenty-two upper caste men
who gang-raped her
and was jailed and freed
at last, after the prison doctors
cut out her womb
for the women who killed
husbands or boyfriends who raped them
and are still in jail

ולכבוד אלו שחמקו,
למען הסבתא
שהכתה זר עד עילפון,
בעזרת הטלפון שנצב על שולחן הלילה,
והסגירה אותו למשטרה.
לכבוד הסטודנטית
שנשכה את לשון התוקף
אשר במו פיו הפליל את עצמו.

לכבוד נשים שלחמו
בכל אשר הן יכלו בזמנן.
למען אמונתן ככל שתהיה,
למען אהבתן למי שתהיה.
לכבוד נשים שהקריבו או הצילו את חייהן
אנו שותות.

תבורך האישה אשר נאבקה למרות זכרונות של מכות והשפלות.
תבורך האישה שחדלה להתנצל על כך שהיא נושמת,
אשר שאפה פחד ונשפה חימה.
תבורך האישה המלמדת את אמנות הלוחם,
אשר בעצם קיומה מאפשרת לאחרות להתחבר למקור כוחן.

and for those who escaped,
the grandma who beat up the stranger
with the phone on her nightstand
who knocked him out and
turned him in, the student
who bit off her attacker's tongue —
his own mouth convicted him

for women who fought however
they could in their time
for whatever they believed
and whoever they loved
who gave their lives or saved them,
we drink.

Blessed is the woman who fought through the memories of beatings and humiliations, who stopped begging pardon for breathing, who inhaled fear and spat fury. Blessed is the woman who teaches the warrior's art, who by example and exhortation enables others to take their own power.

Women teach self-defense techniques at an anti-rape demonstration in Oakland, August 1997. (l to R) Schuyler Fishman, Vanessa Wilson, Martha Shelley, Jen Resnick, Cory Wechsler, Ana Perez (Photo: Associated Press).

HALLEL - GIVING PRAISE

Fill the fourth cup, fill one extra cup, and open the door. Traditionally, the extra cup and open door are to welcome the prophet Elijah, who is supposed to return to earth to herald the coming of the Messiah. At some seders the cup is poured for the prophetess Miriam. Let ours be for the teacher we haven't met yet, someone who will help us obtain whatever gift we longed for when we ate the afikomen.

What shall we praise? If God died in Auschwitz, Whom shall we praise? We live in an age of genocide; it is impossible to believe in a god who punishes people for their sins, because the souls of tens of millions of murdered children would bear witness against him. But we can consider our disbelief in the light of the teachings of Kalonymus Kalman Shapira, rabbi of the Warsaw ghetto. He witnessed the deaths of his family and his entire congregation, his faith was quite literally tested by fire, and his writings were unearthed from the ashes.

He came to believe that God is everywhere, in everything. That the universe as we know it is an illusion. That evil is only a perverted expression of the yearning for unity with the divine. In short, he arrived at the same beliefs the Hindu sages held centuries ago. If we accept this, we can praise the Who and the What in the same breath, for they are One.

Then do we praise the columbine and the crematoria in the same breath? Everything in us revolts against this. Even if the world is God and we are one with God, we do not simply accept what is given, let the hungry starve, bare our throats to the murderers. We are Israel, we wrestle with God. Our tradition says that our duty is *tikkun ha'olam*, repairing the world; in this way we as human beings participate in the act of creation. Or, more modestly, in the Eastern view, we attempt to restore harmony between heaven and earth.

Then should the question be, *why* shall we praise? Maybe because we need to — just as we need to act rather than acquiesce to evil. Maybe this is part of what it means to be human: if we fail to celebrate, heaven and earth won't be diminished — but we will.

> *Praise earth with all your being,*
> *caress her with your dancing,*
>> *with your nakedness stretched full-length*
>> *against black loam or hot sand*
> *praise the wind with each breath*
>> *fill your lungs with the exhalations of trees*
>> *and insects and infants and murderers,*
>> *the same air that Moses and Pharaoh breathed,*
>> *that your enemy breathes, is yours,*
>> *you can't avoid it*
> *get drunk on every lime-green leaf*
>> *or iridescent feather or*
>> *oil slick in the gutter*
> *let every sense embrace the world*
> *let your soul be transparent, let praise*
>> *pour through you like sunlight:*
>
> *whoever loves the earth is forever*
>> *in the presence of the beloved*
>> *will never be bored by her*
>> *never betrayed*
>> *never be lonely.*

לכבוד האנשים הפשוטים
אשר התנגדו לעבדות משחר הימים.

לכבוד המצרייה אשר ידעה שהעברים עוזבים
ובכל זאת נתנה לשכנתה עגיל זהב, נשיקה חפוזה
והליטה את פניה להסתיר את הדמעות.

לכבוד האישה האשורית אשר פתחה את דלתה
וחילקה את פיתה עם העבד הנמלט.
ארזה שאריות דגים ולחם שעורים
ולוותה את ה"אורח" אל מעבר לשערי העיר
ביודעה כי יתכן וילדיה ילקחו לעבדים
כפדיון חוב שלא נפרע.

לכבוד האישה באלבמה אשר פתחה את דלתה
בפני עבדים נמלטים, ריפאה את פצעיהם,
טיגנה עוף ולחם תירס.
הסתירה אותם תחת שמיכות וחציר בעגלת בעלה
אשר הסיעם עד התחנה הבאה בנתיב מחתרת החירות.
בידיעה ברורה כי אם יתגלו יאסרו
וחוותם תועבר לאדון כפצוי.

KOS REVIYIT - FOURTH CUP

Our fourth and final cup is for those women and men whose commitment to justice transcends kinship, or national borders, or the custom of the time.

For the humble whose lives escaped notice, who've
*   resisted slavery since the dawn of history:*

the Egyptian who knew the Hebrews were leaving, who
*   gave her neighbor gold earrings and a quick kiss,*
*   and veiled her face to hide the tears*

the woman in ancient Assyria who opened her door
*   to a slave running away, who shared what she had,*
*   leftover fish and barley bread, and wrapped*
*   the rest in a palm leaf and walked her guest*
*   past the gates of the city, knowing her own children*
*   could be taken to recompense the master*
*   deprived of his property*

the woman in Alabama who opened her door
*   to slaves running away, dressed their wounds,*
*   fried up chicken and corn bread,*
*   tucked them under blankets and hay in the wagon*
*   whose husband rode them north to the next station*
*   on the Underground Railroad, knowing they both*
*   could be imprisoned, their farm taken*
*   to recompense the masters*

לכבוד הגרמנים והפולנים אשר הסתירו יהודים בעליות גג,
זייפו דרכונים ותעודות מסע.
חלקו איתם את הכרוב, תפוחי האדמה וזנב נקניק.
בידיעה ברורה כי אם יתגלו יחלקו גם את אותו הקבר.

לכבוד הכומר המקיים מקלט לבני גוואטמלה
הנמלטים מפלוגות המוות.

לכבוד הסבית המנהלת מקלט לנשים מוכות.
לכבוד אלה אשר בעבור מעשיהם שכניהם שנאום.
לכבוד האישה הלבנה אשר ליוותה ילדים שחורים לבית הספר
דרך המון זועם של אנשי הקלן.
שכניה קראו לה "אוהבת כושים", הביאו לפטורי בעלה,
איימו עליה ברצח, ונפצו את חלונותיה בירירות.

לכבוד הפמיניסטית המוסלמית אשר הגנה
על בני ההינדו מפני מוסלמים אשר אנסו,
ורצחו בהם, שרפו את בתיהם וגזלו את אדמותיהם.
המולות העמידו פרסים עבור ראשה.
שכנותיה קראו לה זונה ודרשו את דמה
והיא נמלטה לארץ זרה.

לכבוד הישראלים אשר הגנו על ערבים מפני יהודים
שעינו אותם, ירו בהם,
הרסו את בתיהם ולקחו את אדמותיהם.
שכניהם כינו אותם שונאי יהודים
והעירו אותם בקריאות גנאי.

the Germans and Poles who hid Jews in the attic,
who forged passports and found them passage
on ships, who shared cabbage and potatoes
and a rationed bit of sausage, knowing if they
were discovered they'd share the same grave,

the deacon who runs a sanctuary for Guatemalans
escaping the death squads,
the dyke who runs a battered women's shelter;

and for those whose neighbors noticed well enough,
and hated them:

the white woman who walked Black children to school
past mobs of screaming Klansmen, whose neighbors called
her niggerlover, got her husband fired, phoned
them with death threats, shot through their windows

the Muslim feminist who defended Hindus against Muslims
who raped and murdered them, burned their homes
and took their land, and the mullahs put a price
on her head and the neighbors called her a slut
and demanded her blood, and she escaped into exile

the Israelis who defended Arabs against Jews
who tortured them, shot them, bulldozed their homes
and took their land, and the neighbors called them
self-hating Jews and woke them with obscene calls

לכבוד האישה אשר דיברה בשם היערות כנגד אנשים
והתאגידים תת אנושיים אשר כרתו הכריתו וחרשו אותם.
שכניה קראו לה חובבת עצים הגוזלת את פרנסתם,
מכוניתה פוצצה וכן חצי גופה.

לכבוד האישה אשר שכניה אמרו עליה היא קולנית, משוגעת
סקסית מדי היא ניראית כמו זונה או מכוערת מדי,
לעולם לא תמצא גבר, היא עושה צרות כי היא לסבית.
החבר שלה הביא אותה לכך.

לכבוד הגבר אשר סרב להרוג וקוראים לו הומו.
הגבר אשר לא יגזול מדל וקוראים לו בוגד.
הגבר אשר משליך את גופו אל מול הטנקים,
במקום לכתוב מכתבים למערכת וקוראים לו מחבל.

לכבוד כל אלה שמעולם לא ראינו
וכל אלה שלא יכולנו לא לראות,
לכבוד כל הנשים והגברים שהסתכנו במאסר, גרוש או מוות.
אנו שותות.

שמע ישראל!
לא המשיח אלא, מעטים אלה, הבלתי מושלמים בכל דור ודור
באומץ ליבם הביאו לכם את הגאולה.

the woman who spoke for the forests against humans
and the inhuman corporations who bulldozed and chainsawed
and clear-cut them, and the neighbors called her a
treehugger taking their jobs, and her car was bombed
and her body half blown away;

for the woman whose neighbors say she's shrill or crazy
or too sexy—she looks like a whore, or too ugly—
she can't get a man, she makes trouble because
she's a dyke, because her boyfriend put her up to it;

for the man who will not kill and is called a fag, who will
not rob the poor and is called a traitor, who hurls
his own body against the tanks instead of writing letters
to the editor, and is called a terrorist

for those we never saw and those we could not fail to see,
for all the women and men who risk imprisonment, exile
or death, for righteousness' sake, we drink.

Hear O Israel!
it is not the Messiah but these
imperfect few, in every generation,
whose courage has redeemed you.

Drink the last cup, again reclining on the left side.

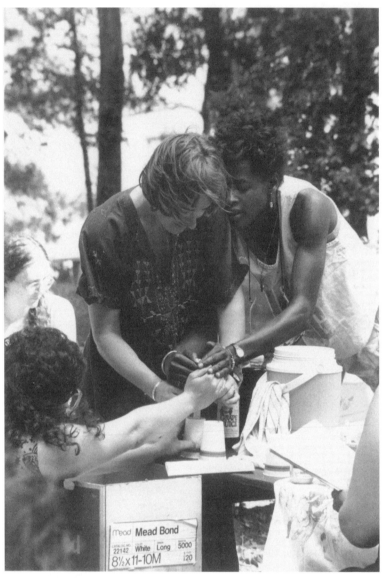
**Women conducting a seder at the 1992 Gulf Coast Women's Music Festival.
(Photo: Toni Armstrong Jr.)**

NIRTZAH - ALL IS ACCEPTED

We have completed the seder according to our best under-standing, in the spirit of our desire for freedom and justice. May all we have done be blessed. And because the name *Jerusalem* means "city of peace", let us say with our ancestors,

L'shana haba'a b'Yerushalayim! — Next year in Jerusalem!

לשנה הבאה בירושלים הבנויה

aunt lute books is a multicultural women's press that has been committed to publishing high quality, culturally diverse literature since 1982. In 1990, the Aunt Lute Foundation was formed as a non-profit corporation to publish and distribute books that reflect the complex truths of women's lives and the possibilities for personal and social change. We seek work that explores the specificities of the very different histories from which we come, and that examines the intersections between the borders we all inhabit.

Please write or phone if you would like us to send you a free catalog of our other books or if you wish to be on our mailing list for future titles. You may buy books directly from us by phoning in a credit card order or mailing a check with the catalog order form.

Aunt Lute Books
P.O.Box 410687
San Francisco, CA 94141
(415)826-1300
www.best.com/~auntlute/

This book would not have been possible without the kind contributions of the Aunt Lute Founding Friends:

Anonymous Donor	Diana Harris
Anonymous Donor	Phoebe Robins Hunter
Rusty Barcelo	Diane Mosbacher, M.D., Ph.D.
Marian Bremer	William Preston, Jr.
Diane Goldstein	Elise Rymer Turner